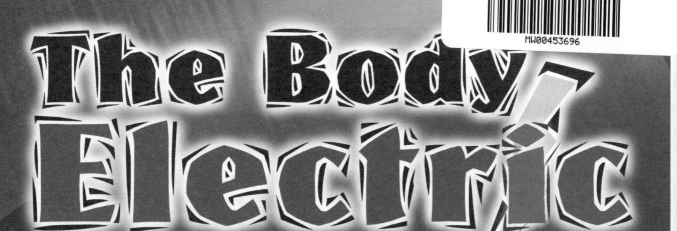

The Body Electric

A Symphony of Sounds for Body Percussion

Mark Burrows

Dedicated to Dr. B.

Editor: Kris Kropff

Cover and Book Design: Jeff Richards

Music Engraving: Linda Taylor

CD Producer: Mark Burrows

Recorded, mixed and mastered by Bart Rose at First Street Audio, Ft. Worth, Texas
Special thanks to Mandy Hoak, Patrick Hood and Maddie McClung for sharing their talents on the recording.

Heritage Music Press a division of The Lorenz Corporation
P.O. Box 802 Dayton, Ohio 45401
www.lorenz.com

Printed in the United States of America

ISBN: 978-0-89328-439-8

HMP
HERITAGE MUSIC PRESS
A Division of The Lorenz Corporation
Box 802 / Dayton, OH 45401-0802
www.lorenz.com

Contents

ntroduction

Have you ever been to a band or orchestra rehearsal and watched the percussionists? They're fun to watch. Envision them for a second. While the other musicians must sit in chairs, the percussionists are dashing from instrument to instrument, often with only a measure or two to get where they're headed. Then the conductor stops to work on a bowing or tonguing issue. Are you still watching the percussionists? See what they're doing? They're drumming their knees, tapping their sides, bobbing their heads. They can stop playing the instruments, but the music goes on—because the music is in *them*, not the instruments.

The Body Electric celebrates the music inside us all while exploring ways to express this music using the greatest instruments of all—our bodies.

Here are a few benefits of using body percussion and mouth/vocal sounds.

1. **Convenient.** An entire instrumentarium, complete with carrying case, goes wherever you go.

2. **Inexpensive.** While it's great to have a variety of musical instruments, filling your room with these instruments may be cost prohibitive. Imagine having a whole symphony of sound possibilities without spending a dime.

3. **Physical.** The gestures required to produce many body percussion sounds encourage movement. This can make the transition to dance a whole lot easier, especially for those who may be self conscious about dancing or moving in front of their peers.

4. **Adaptable.** Body percussion rhythms can be put together to form everything from percussion pieces to accompaniment for songs, chants, raps, or rhymes.

5. **Self-Affirming.** It's not easy to put yourself out there. Have you ever noticed how the same people who love music can become incredibly self conscious when asked to sing? When we sing, we become the musician *and* the instrument. The inner critic asks, "If they don't like the way I sing, does it mean they don't like me?" Body percussion and vocal/mouth sounds allow us put ourselves "out there" in less obvious ways, which could lead to greater self confidence later on.

6. **Educational.** Body percussion and vocal sounds heighten the ability to internalize rhythmic concepts.

7. **Fun.** Don't forget fun! This is absolutely crucial. We represent the last formal music training many of our students will ever have. If we can create an environment where our students come to love music, they stand a much greater chance of choosing music for themselves later on. If they *love* it, they'll *learn* it. The reverse is not necessarily true.

The Raspberry Factor

When exploring sounds the body can make, it's only a matter of time before someone decides to perform a raspberry. My little brother and I were especially good at raspberries and had many different methods depending on our mood at the time.

You are perfectly within your rights to declare your room a "No-Raspberry Zone." However, the occasional well-placed raspberry can be quite effective in a body percussion piece, and will undoubtedly win you valuable points with your students—points you may need later. Just think about it.

How to Use this Resource

There's no need to read *The Body Electric* cover to cover. It's a handy reference, even an idea-generator, not the next great American novel. Use what you need when you need it.

The material is organized in three main sections:
1. Stomp, Pat, Clap, Snap: The "Big Four" of Body Percussion
2. The Human Voice: A World of Possibilities
3. Click, Clap, Say, Stomp, Pop, and Pat: The Whole Body Electric

General information as well as targeted examples for a variety of body, vocal and mouth sounds are included within the first two sections. The last section includes pieces that employ various combinations of all the sounds presented in *The Body Electric*.

This resource contains numerous musical examples. Don't feel that you must adhere strictly to every little eighth note. The musical examples represent one way, not the only way. In fact this resource is incomplete if not combined with your and your students' creativity.

Here are but a few ways you can take what's written and make it "your own."

1. Add variety to a piece through changes in dynamics. You can indicate a *crescendo* by gradually raising your outstretched arm with the palm up. Do the reverse to indicate a *decrescendo*.

2. Choose a point in a piece of music for a call-and-response or echo section. A soloist or small group can play a rhythm that is either responded to or directly echoed. What's the difference? An echo is playing verbatim the rhythm just played. In call-and-response, the response is usually different material than the call. If "Shave and a haircut" is the call, what is the response? (Two bits.)

3. Add variety to a piece through changes in tone color. A rhythm in one part could be stomped for eight measures then snapped for eight measures.

4. Put a piece together in performance using the layering process. Start with one part then gradually add each part until all parts are playing. Take the piece through changes in dynamics and end on a strong downbeat. Or end the piece the same way you started, silencing parts one at a time until only one remains.

5. Allow for improvisation. Kids are extremely creative, and many will welcome the chance to perform a rhythmic improvisation. Many of the musical examples in this resource are "groove oriented" (they have a continuous, repetitive intensity), and thus lend themselves to serving as foundations for improvisations.

6. In some cases free rhythm is appropriate. For example, if the students are creating a soundscape or a soundtrack to a famous painting, strict rhythms may not work as well.

7. Make substitutions whenever and wherever you like. The suggestions for each part in a given musical example are just that—suggestions. If there is another body percussion or vocal/mouth sound that works better in your setting, by all means, go with it!

8. Have the students compose their own pieces using the musical examples in the resource for inspiration.

9. Modify the pieces to fit a particular age group. Don't feel that a class of second graders must perform all parts of a piece. Extract two or three parts that the students can perform successfully.

CD Information

The CD included with *The Body Electric* may be used in a number of ways. Examples of the sounds introduced in this resource are presented as a model for your students. Most of the pieces are performed using the layering process. This gradual addition of parts is a wonderful way to utilize the pieces in this collection. In this way, the CD serves as an excellent model of performance options. Your students may also clap, snap, pop, speak and move along with the pieces on the CD to help keep the steady beat and for added part security.

Track point indications are provided throughout this resource. In some cases, we have provided additional details like the number of repetitions, as well as the formal structure used on the recording. In addition to providing a concrete option for that piece, remember that the same concept will likely work with other pieces in this collection, as well as other rhythmic patterns you or your students create.

CD Tracks

1. Introduction
2. Making Rain

Palmas
3. I
4. II
5. III

Body Percussion Solos
6. Solo 1
7. Solo 2
8. Solo 3
9. Solo 4
10. Body Percussion—West African

Lip Pops and Tongue Clicks
11. The Fish
12. The Popgun
13. The Hand Pop
14. The Horse
15. The Baseball
16. Temple Block
17. The Chipmunk
18. Making Popcorn

Alpha-beat Soup
19. Voiced
20. Unvoiced

Beatboxing
21. Big crash cymbal
22. Small crash cymbal
23. Hi-hat
24. Bass drum
25. Bass drum (electronic)
26. Snare
27. Techno-snare
28. Toms
29. Scratch record
30. Native-American drum
31. Techno bass drum

Beatbox Solos
32. Techno-beat
33. Rock
34. Rock II
35. Waltz

36. Group Beatbox
37. Poetry Slam: How Doth the Little Crocodile
38. Sound Machine
39. Barnyard Bash
40. Salutation Samba
41. Planet Jam
42. Body Percussion—Cuban
43. I Hear America Singing
44. The Body Electric

Stomp, Pat, Clap, Snap: The "Big Four" of Body Percussion

The term "body percussion" usually calls to mind four main gestures: stomping, patting, clapping, and snapping. These simple, natural gestures are vital to the music of many world cultures, and have been for centuries. But because of the initial simplicity of these gestures, we often underestimate their value. I wish I could take back all the times when I told students that if they didn't have drums they could "just" pat their knees. Or if they didn't have tambourines they could "just" clap their hands.

The truth is that despite all the technological developments of musical instruments through the years, many cultures still *choose* to use body percussion. Perhaps it's because of the freedom of movement these gestures allow. Or it could be because each gesture produces a tone that simply cannot be replicated by an instrument. One thing is certain—each gesture contains an incredible array of unique sounds, which should be enough to convince anyone to drop the word "just" when referring to body percussion.

1. Stomping

From Irish clogging to African-American stepping, the stomp (or its cousin, the tap) has proven to be a powerful musical gesture. One of the reasons stomping is popular in so many cultures is its efficient combination of music and movement. Think of how stimulating a tap dance performance can be both visually and aurally.

Stomping may also have been one of the first ways musicians kept time. The rhythmical stomping of the fiddler at a hoedown is as much a part of the musical experience as the melody played on the fiddle itself.

Have the students explore some of the many sound possibilities of stomping:

1. Stomp with the whole foot.
2. Stomp with the heel only.
3. Tap with the toes only.
4. Stomp with both feet at the same time. (This requires either jumping or sitting in a chair.)
5. Have all the students stomp at the same time.
6. Have only a few students stomp.
7. Have the students stomp one at a time.
8. Experiment with different combinations of heel, toe and whole-foot stomping.

Many cultures, particularly in the South Pacific, dig holes in the ground and lay wooden planks across the tops, creating stamping pits. Have the students explore the variety of sounds produced by stomping on different surfaces. How will the sound be affected by a floor with carpet? Wood? Concrete? Linoleum? Even the material on the soles of the shoes can produce significantly different sounds.

Other body percussion options for feet include clicking the heels together and shuffling the feet on the floor, as in soft-shoe dancing.

2. Clapping

Clapping is a universal form of expression that can be as simple as clapping to the beat or as complex as the intricate *palmas* rhythms found in Spanish flamenco music. Clapping can also offer an opportunity to make music with a partner, as in numerous African and African-American clapping games. There are almost as many different sounds as there are functions for clapping. The following are a few of the possibilities:

1. Clap with both hands cupped.
2. Clap with both hands flat.
3. Clap with one hand cupped, and the other flat.
4. Clap with the heels of the hands only.
5. Clap with the pads of the fingers only.
6. Clap with only two fingers of each hand.
7. Clap with the backs of the hands.
8. Clap with the fingertips only.
9. Clap the pads of the fingers of one hand into the palm of the other.
10. Clap the pads of the spread-apart fingers of one hand into the palm of the other, creating a splattered or "wet" sound.

Divide the students into pairs and have them explore the possibilities of partner clapping. Have the students change partners and take note of how each pairing produces a slightly (or not-so-slightly) different sound.

Another body percussion option for hands is to rub them together, creating a soft friction sound.

3. Patting

Rhythmic patting (sometimes called "patschen") can be found in everything from Alpine folk dances to the Samoan "slap dance," *fa 'ataupati* (fah ah-tau-PAH-tee). In patting, the body is a veritable orchestra, offering many unique sound possibilities. Here are a few:

1. Pat the thighs.
2. Pat the knees.
3. Pat the tummy.
4. Pat the chest.
5. Pat the backs of the legs.
6. Pat the forearms.
7. Pat the shoulders.

Different combinations of pats can be put together to create exciting, infectious rhythms, as in African-American *juba* music. Invite the students to explore the many sound possibilities, reminding them to treat their bodies, like all other valuable musical instruments, with respect. Music isn't supposed to hurt!

4. Snapping

It's virtually impossible to imagine jazz without the rhythmic snapping on the backbeat. Snapping is also integral to the frantic Bhangra dance of India. Whether with one hand or two, snaps can add wonderful color to a body percussion piece.

Offer an alternative for those students (often younger ones) who find it difficult to snap.

Making Rain

This is a fun body percussion activity which requires no attention to specific rhythms. Have the students watch and perform with you the following sequence of sounds:

1. Rub hands together (5 seconds)
2. Snaps (5 seconds)
3. Pat thighs softly (5 seconds)
4. Pat thighs louder (5 seconds)
5. Clap softly (5 seconds)
6. Clap louder (10 seconds)
7. During loud clapping, make thunder sounds vocally
8. Clap softly (5 seconds)
9. Pat thighs loudly (5 seconds)
10. Pat thighs softer (5 seconds)
11. Snaps (5 seconds)
12. Rub hands together (5 seconds)

Don't feel the need to adhere rigidly to the time suggestions. Your rain may vary. You may even choose to put another swell or two into the stormier sections.

Pat-a-Cake: Body Percussion Disguised as a Game

There are many street rhymes and finger plays from around the world that are basically chants with body percussion. Clapping games, from the European rhyme *Pease Porridge Hot* to the West African song *Sorida*, combine rhythm and rhyme with a teamwork aspect.

The following is a simple clapping pattern which can accompany literally thousands of rhymes. Divide the students into pairs and have the students of each pair face each other. Teach the following clapping patterns:

Pattern 1:

Clap own hands.
Clap partner's hands.
Clap back of hands to back of partner's hands.
Clap partner's hands.

Pattern 2:

Clap own hands.
Clap partner's right hand with your right hand.
Clap own hands.
Clap partner's left hand with your left hand.

Perform Pattern 1 twice, then Pattern 2, then repeat Pattern 1.
If time allows, have the pairs create a new pattern.

Page 10 includes a few samples of *palmas*, the rhythmic clapping found in Spanish flamenco music and dance. This particular activity has the benefit of teaching students the difference between the steady beat and the melodic rhythm, as well as how the two can work together.

Process

1. Divide the students into two groups.

2. Teach each group one of the rhythm parts from the palmas of your choice.

3. When teaching the different parts, have each part clap with a different tone color. For example, have one group clap with cupped hands while the other group claps with flat hands. (See the list on page 7 for other suggestions.)

4. Each palmas rhythm may also be performed as a rhythmic duet between two players.

Note: Palmas III has two distinct rhythms. One is a steady stream of quarter notes while the other is the rhythm made by counting to ten in Spanish.

CD Information: Palmas I and II are each performed four times on the CD. Palmas III is performed twice. Part I of that palmas is clapped only so can accompany the spoken part. All are performed at ♩ = 120.

Pronuciation Guide

uno	OO-no
dos	dohs
tres	trehs
cuatro	QUAH-troh
cinco	SEEN-koh
seis	saçe (rhymes with face)
siete	sea EH-teh
ocho	OH-cho
nueve	noo EH-veh
diez	dyehs

Extension

These palmas patterns work best when accompanying a song. Entire palmas pieces can be performed by having one group clap steady quarter notes while the other group claps the rhythm to a familiar song.

Palmas

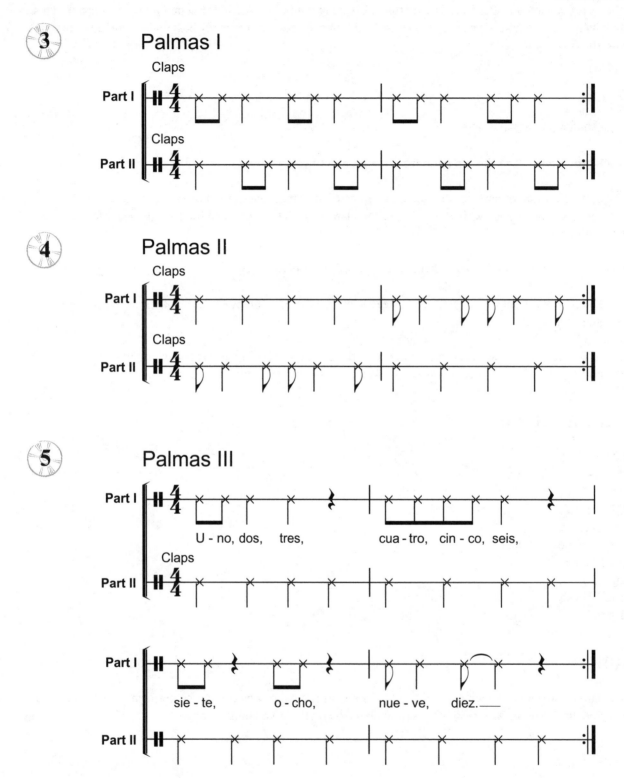

Palmas I

Palmas II

Palmas III

U - no, dos, tres, cua - tro, cin - co, seis,

sie - te, o - cho, nue - ve, diez.

A few rhythms which can be performed as body percussion solos are offered below.

First, have the students explore body percussions they can perform. Then, ask the students to stand in a circle. Allow each student 4 measures (16 beats if in $\frac{4}{4}$) to improvise a body percussion solo.

Some of these improvisations can be featured as solos in other pieces, or these rhythms may be put together to form a stand-alone solo piece. Like beatboxing (introduced on page 20), these rhythms work very well when accompanying a song, chant or rap.

CD Information: Solos 1, 2 and 4 are each repeated four times. Solo 3 is performed as written.

Body Percussion—West African

Body Percussion—West African is a piece patterned after certain West African drumming rhythms. While "West African" is an impossibly broad term, there are a few characteristics which distinguish West African rhythms from rhythms in other world cultures. One element of interest is the frequent use of *polyrhythm*. This often happens when a triplet rhythm (♩ + ♩ + ♩) is overlaid with a rhythm in duple (♩. + ♩.). The result is a piece with a rich rhythmic texture, as well as a sense of forward momentum.

This piece has been written out to illustrate one performance possibility. As with every piece, feel free to adapt *Body Percussion—West African* to your particular needs.

Process

1. Divide the students into four groups.

2. Teach each group one of the four parts, then bring in each group as indicated in the music. Each part has a rhythm A and a rhythm B. The measure in which this rhythmic change occurs is marked in the part with an "*".

3. You may teach the parts by rote, or reproduce the page of 2-bar figures for each part found on page 15. (You'll need to signal each group so they know when to switch from rhythm A to rhythm B.)

Extension

This piece provides a good illustration of the need for space in groove-based percussion music. As in conversation, each individual part must provide enough space for the other parts to "speak." This is important to keep in mind when having the students create their own percussion pieces. Oftentimes a player will hear an entire piece in his or her head and try to play all the parts at once.

Have the students observe how the moments of space in each part of *Body Percussion—West African* help to keep the piece from becoming too cluttered. Note also that the amount of space in each part decreases at each of the "*" spots. This gives the piece the feeling of speeding up without increasing the tempo.

Body Percussion—West African

Mark Burrows

Body Percussion—West African

Mark Burrows

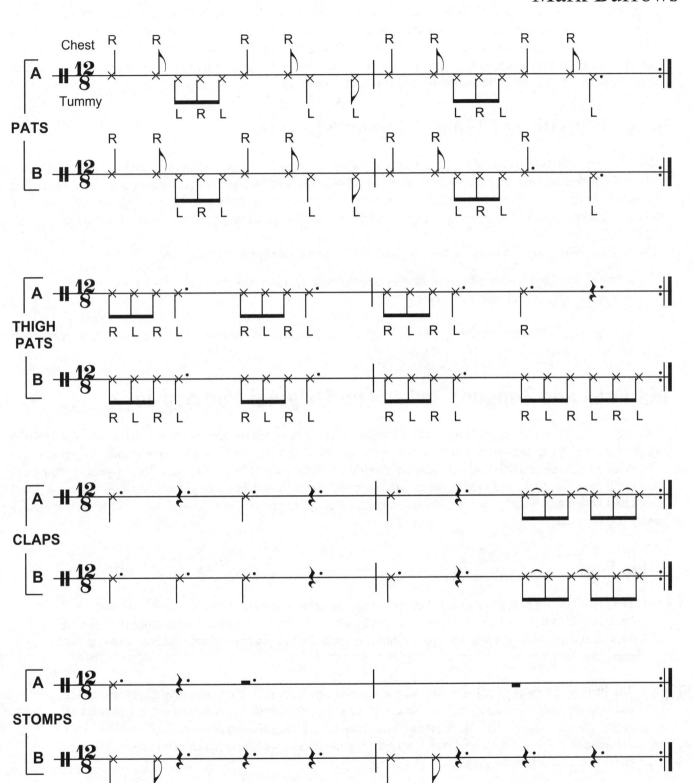

The Human Voice: A World of Possibilities

Since percussion instruments are usually defined as those which may be struck, shaken or scraped, we often forget about the percussive possibilities of the human voice. Many world cultures use their voices as much for percussion as they do for singing. Often called "vocal percussion," this term is a bit of a misnomer. There are many percussive sounds created by the mouth, tongue and lips that do not involve the vocal chords at all. There are also many sounds that can be made by combining the mouth and hands or fingers.

Sing, Whistle and Hum: Melody Matters

When dealing with body music, we often get stuck thinking in terms only of percussion. But the body is also an instrument with incredible melodic potential. For many world cultures, singing and body percussion go hand in hand (pun intended). In many instances it would be unthinkable to perform body percussion without a song. You can also add a whole new element to a body percussion piece through the addition of a melody, either whistled or hummed.

The addition of melody to a body percussion piece can be approached in numerous ways:

- A few students could hum, whistle or sing an existing melody. Then add other students on body percussion parts that complement the melody.

- Another way is to establish a body percussion rhythm. Then choose one student to hum or whistle an improvised melody inspired by the rhythms.

Lip Pops and Tongue Clicks: The Original Pop Music

There are many different kinds of lip pops and tongue clicks, all of which use the mouth as a resonator. The position of the mouth plays an important role in affecting the volume, pitch and tone color of each sound. As you perform the following sounds, experiment with different mouth positions such as "ah," "oh," and "oo." Opening the mouth more will raise the pitch, and closing the mouth more will lower the pitch. Some sounds, such as "the horse," will work best with a combination of high and low clicks. In fact, given practice, it is possible to play complete melodies using pops or clicks.

Lip Pops:

11 1. **The Fish.** This lip pop gets its name because of the aquarium-bubble-like sound created. Oh yeah, and because you look like a fish when you do it. No hands or fingers are needed. Simply close the lips and suck in slightly while keeping the lips sealed. Then pull the lips apart to release the seal and create a pop.

12 2. **The Popgun.** Done correctly, this pop will sound just like a popgun. Put your index finger just inside your mouth against the inside of the cheek. Create a seal around the finger with the lips and build up pressure behind the seal by inflating the cheeks. Then quickly flick the finger out of the mouth, breaking the seal and creating a nice, loud pop. It's always a good idea to wash your hands before trying the popgun, or at least your index finger.

13 3. **The Hand Pop.** Open your mouth to an "oh" position. Keep the lips relaxed as you gently pat the "oh" with the finger pads of one hand.

Tongue Clicks:

14   1. **The Horse.** This tongue click gets its name because it emulates the sound of a horse's hooves. Pull the tip of the tongue half way back to the roof of the mouth. Create a suction seal between the tongue and the roof of the mouth. Then pull the tongue down, breaking the seal and creating a distinct clicking sound. Perform this click several times in a row. Make the horse speed up or slow down by changing the tempo of your clicks.

15   2. **The Baseball.** This tongue click can produce a loud, sharp sound similar to a baseball being hit. Push the tip of the tongue right behind the teeth at the roof of the mouth. Create a strong suction seal between the tip of the tongue and the roof of the mouth. Build up more suction by pulling the back of the tongue down slightly. Then abruptly break the seal by dropping the jaw and thrusting the tongue to the floor of the mouth.

Getting Cheeky:

16   1. **Temple Block.** Open the mouth to an "oh" position. Using the pads of the fingers, gently tap the cheeks to create a temple block sound.

17   2. **The Chipmunk.** This fun sound effect may take some practice. Store a pocket of air in one cheek, behind the teeth. Keep the mouth as open as possible without losing this pocket. Then gently tap on the cheek with the finger tips so the air will "squirt" over the teeth, creating a chipmunk sound.

Making Popcorn   **18**

This is a fun mouth percussion activity with no specific rhythms.

Have the students sit with you in a circle on the floor. Point to a student and indicate for him or her to make slow, continuous lip pops. Point to another student, then another, until all the students are making lip pops.

Once all the students are popping, have them pop faster and faster until it sounds like popcorn popping. Then, one by one, point to a student and indicate for him or her to stop popping until all that remains is one "kernel."

Alpha-Beats

The alphabet is rich with wonderful, colorful percussive sounds. Each letter has its own character, from the explosive "B" to the warm "V."

Voiced consonants are those which use the vocal chords, and so contain pitch. Unvoiced consonants use the articulators (lips, teeth, tongue) without the aid of the voice, and so do not contain pitch. Below are some of the English language consonants. Where possible, the unvoiced consonant is shown next to its voiced cousin.

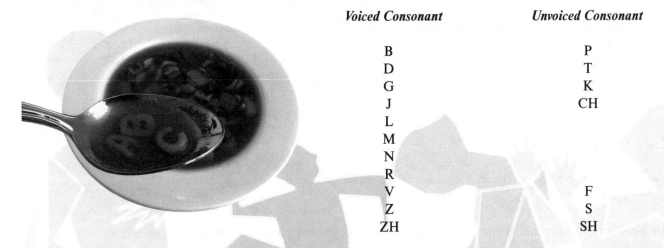

Voiced Consonant	Unvoiced Consonant
B	P
D	T
G	K
J	CH
L	
M	
N	
R	
V	F
Z	S
ZH	SH

Experiment with different consonants and consonant combinations. Mix and match to find cool, new sounds.

- Try using different pitches to affect the sound of the voiced consonants.

- Try different mouth positions to give each consonant a different resonance. For example, an "uh" vowel formation will make a vocalized "D" sound deeper and richer. An "ih" vowel formation will make a vocalized "D" sound brighter.

Experiment with consonant sounds from non-English languages. Here are a few examples:

- Rolled "R" (Italian, Spanish)

- Guttural "CH" (German)

- Glottal, which is produced by the quick release of built-up air behind the vocal folds. (Found in the Chinese dialect of *Tsou*)

Name Game

Don't overlook the wonderful rhythms and tones that exist in the students' names. Using them to create an original piece is a great way to illustrate how every child is important and brings something irreplaceable to their community. Each child's name offers something unique to the whole. Even when two students have the same name, the way they express it tonally and rhythmically may be very different. Without each individual contributing what they have and what they are, the piece simply won't be the same.

Alpha-beat Soup

Mark Burrows

The following are two rhythm patterns utilizing the sounds of different consonants. One rhythm uses three different voiced consonants while the other highlights three unvoiced consonants. These rhythms can serve as accompaniments for rhymes, chants or songs. They may also serve as stand-alone percussion pieces by adding other alphabet sounds.

The two rhythms may also be combined into one piece. This can be achieved by having the students chant the voiced rhythm for several measures, then switching to the unvoiced rhythm for several more measures. Then, the students can switch back to the voiced rhythm and finish the piece.

CD Information: The examples on the CD show one performance option for these patterns—using the layering process to create a 16-measure piece. Begin with Part 1 alone, and repeat. Add Part 2 and perform together twice. Add Part 3 and perform all parts four times. Be sure to cue a strong cutoff. A recommended tempo for this piece is ♩ = 112.

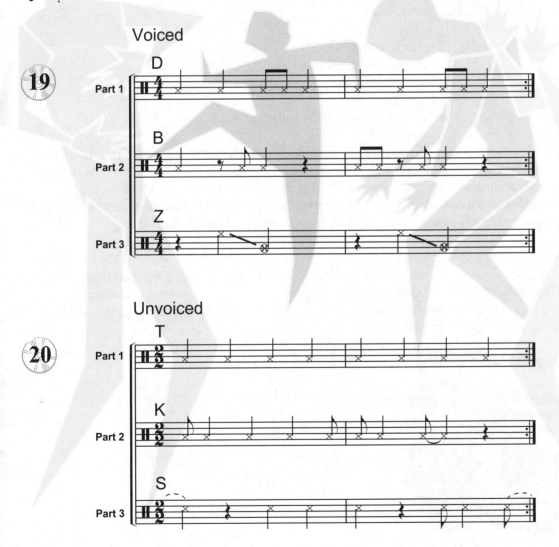

Beatboxing

Over the past few decades hip-hop has emerged as a powerful force in the world of popular music. As hip-hop has developed, so has the art of vocal percussion known as *beatboxing*. Beatboxing often uses consonants and consonant clusters to imitate the sounds of drums, cymbals and even scratch records.

The following are some common beatboxing sounds and the instruments they imitate. The examples on the CD begin with track 21 and progress in the order below. Each sound is announced at the beginning of the track.

Beatboxing Sound	Instrument
Psh	big crash cymbal
Ksh	small crash cymbal
Ts	hi-hat
D(uh)	bass drum
G(uh)	bass drum (electronic)
Kh	snare
Chk	techno-snare
D(ih)-g(ah) d(ih)-g(ah) [high to low]	toms
Wh(ih)k(uh)-wh(ih)k(uh)-wh(ih)k	scratch record
Bm or Dm	Native-American drum
Glottal*	techno bass drum

This glottal is performed with the tongue against the teeth at the roof of the mouth.

These beatboxing sounds are traditionally performed by one person while another chants or raps a text. Okay, I said it. Rap...they rap the text. Mention the words "rap" or "hip-hop" and you're bound to elicit a strong response. Detractors will point to the occasional negative messages presented in the text. Supporters will point out the rhythmic vitality and cultural relevance of rap and hip-hop. If the text seems to be the major stumbling block, choose your own text, such as a famous poem or nursery rhyme. You could even have students rap the times tables.

The facing page includes a few beatbox samples for solo voice, as well as a four-part Group Beatbox. The Group Beatbox performance on the CD is another example of building a piece through layering. Part 1 moves directly from the intro into the groove. They perform the two-bar rhythm four times. Part 2 enters and the parts are performed together four times through. Add Part 3, then 4, in 8-measure intervals. Perform a second eight-measure section with all parts together and bring the piece to a close. A suggested tempo is ♩ = 116.

Beatbox Solos

Mark Burrows

32 Techno-beat

Ts
Glottal

33 Rock

Kh
Dm

34 Rock II

Kh
Dm

(Dih-ga dih-ga dih-ga)

35 Waltz

Chk
Bm

Group Beatbox

Mark Burrows

36 **Intro:**

Part 1

Dih-ga dih-ga Dih-ga dih-ga Dih-ga dih-ga Dih-ga dih-ga

Groove:

Part 1

Dm dm kh dm dm kh   Dm dm kh dm dm kh

Part 2

Ksh   Ksh

Part 3

Bih-dih   bih-dih   bip bip   bih-dih   bih-dih   bip bip

Part 4

Vt, vt,   v———— t, vt   vt, vt,   v———— t, vt

Poetry Slam: How Doth the Little Crocodile

Combine beatboxing and rap with classic poetry. Divide the students into two groups. Have one group perform the beatbox while the other group chants *How Doth the Little Crocodile* in rhythm. Then, have the groups switch parts.

Try the following extension, particularly with your older students:

- Divide the students into pairs. Hand each pair an index card with a short, classic poem. (Pages 45–48 include plenty of examples to get you started.)

- Have the students in each pair find the rhythm inherent in the poem and compose a beatbox to accompany a rhythmic reading of the poem.

- Have the pairs rap/beatbox their poems for the others.

- Afterwards, combine the rapper of one poem with the beatboxer of another. Does the beatbox seem to complement the poem or distract from it?

Poetry Slam: How Doth the Little Crocodile

Mark Burrows
Words by Lewis Carroll (1832-1898)

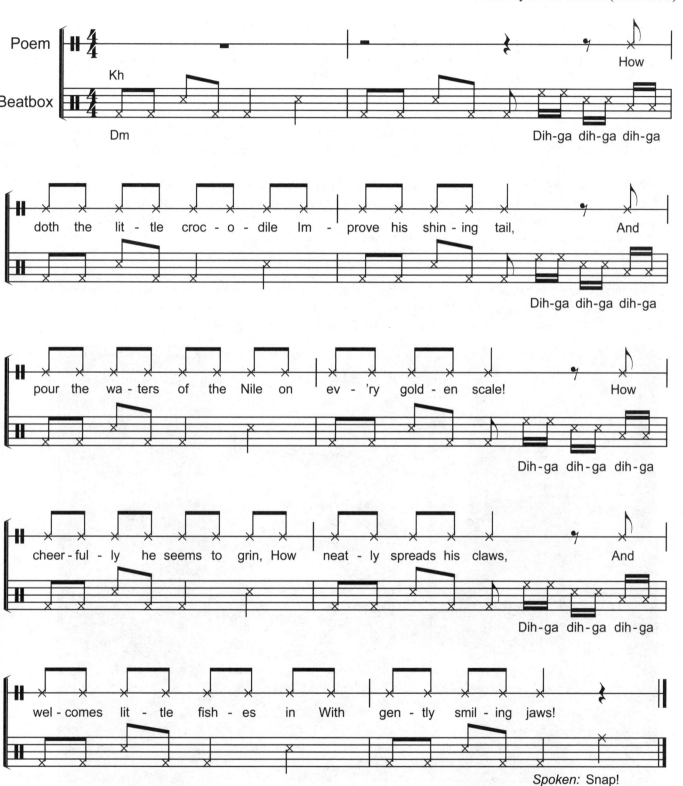

The Sound Machine

The Sound Machine is a vocal/mouth percussion piece based on various mechanical sounds.

Consider the given rhythms and sounds to be merely a starting point. In fact, a fun classroom activity is to have the students create their own Sound Machine. Start by having the students sit in a circle on the floor. Choose one student to stand in the center and perform a simple, repetitive motion while accompanying that motion with a mechanical sound.

While that student continues to perform his or her motion and sound, choose another student to stand next to the first, contributing a new motion and corresponding sound. Do this until all the students are standing together, each contributing his or her own unique motion and sound to the Sound Machine.

Once the Sound Machine has been running for awhile, get everyone's attention with a gesture, such as tapping your nose. Then end the piece with a good, strong cutoff on the downbeat. Another option could be to allow the Sound Machine to breakdown on its own (as most machines eventually do). (The performance example on the CD is treated in this way. After layering the parts over the course of seven repeats, the machine breaks down.)

In performance, rather than having the students sit in a circle on the floor, have them enter one at a time from offstage. They can stand side by side in one long row, like an assembly line, facing the audience. This staging makes *The Sound Machine* a prime candidate for "show opener."

The Sound Machine

Mark Burrows

Tongue clicks

Imitation Fascination

The human voice is an amazing instrument. It has the ability to communicate through speech, song and, as has just been shown, percussive effects. Not to be overlooked is the voice's ability to imitate literally millions of sounds in the world around us.

Listen to as many sounds as you can. Try to find the characteristics that make each sound unique. As you imitate each sound, try to highlight these characteristics. For example, a duck sound is about more than just saying "quack." There is a nasal quality as well. In fact, this nasal quality is so apparent that when Sergei Prokofiev wrote his immensely popular *Peter and the Wolf*, he chose the nasal sound of the oboe to depict the duck.

Here are a few categories and examples of sound possibilities. These sounds, from natural to mechanical to musical, can be used in countless combinations to create original pieces of music.

Barnyard Animals

1. Cow
2. Sheep
3. Pig
4. Duck
5. Rooster
6. Donkey
7. Horse
8. Turkey
9. Goat
10. Chicken

African Animals

1. Lion
2. Elephant
3. Gorilla
4. Hyena
5. Chimpanzee
6. Cobra

Amazon Rainforest Animals

1. Howler monkey
2. Harpy eagle
3. Emerald tree boa
4. Tree frog
5. Jaguar
6. Three-toed sloth
7. Macaw

Vehicle Sounds

1. Car
2. Airplane
3. Rocket
4. Helicopter
5. Train
6. Tug boat

Mechanical Sounds

1. Clock
2. Typewriter
3. Copy machine
4. Washer/Dryer
5. Hair dryer
6. Conveyor belt
7. Alarm clock
8. Telephone

Musical Instruments

1. Flute
2. Oboe
3. Bassoon
4. Trumpet
5. Trombone
6. Tuba
7. Violin
8. Cello
9. Upright bass
10. Electric guitar
11. Triangle
12. Sand blocks
13. Rattles
14. Banjo

Barnyard Bash is a piece for vocal percussion based on the sounds made by various barnyard animals. (Teach the parts by rote, or reproduce page 29, which includes the figures used in Sections A and B.)

The piece starts with an introduction by the rooster. This is to be done free of tempo. Then, at Section A, the parts may be brought in one at a time or by groups. For example, you may bring in all the birds, then all the mammals. Section A has no set duration. Allow the students time to get comfortable in the groove. Then give a signal, such as tapping your nose, to let the students know it is almost time to move on to Section B.

When all eyes are on you, give a solid downbeat to indicate the beginning of Section B. This section is in call-and-response form. It starts with all the barnyard birds giving the call and all the barnyard mammals giving the response. After four measures, the mammals give the call and the birds give the response. Four measures later, return to Section A.

Allow the students to groove in Section A for a while. Then, get their attention and give a cutoff, preferably on a strong downbeat. (The piece is performed this way on the CD, at a tempo of ♩ = 104).

Did you notice that the rhythm for the call and response in Section B is *Old MacDonald?* The call is "Old MacDonald had a farm," and the response is "E-i-e-i-o."

Barnyard Bash

Mark Burrows

*Rolled "R"

Barnyard Bash

Mark Burrows

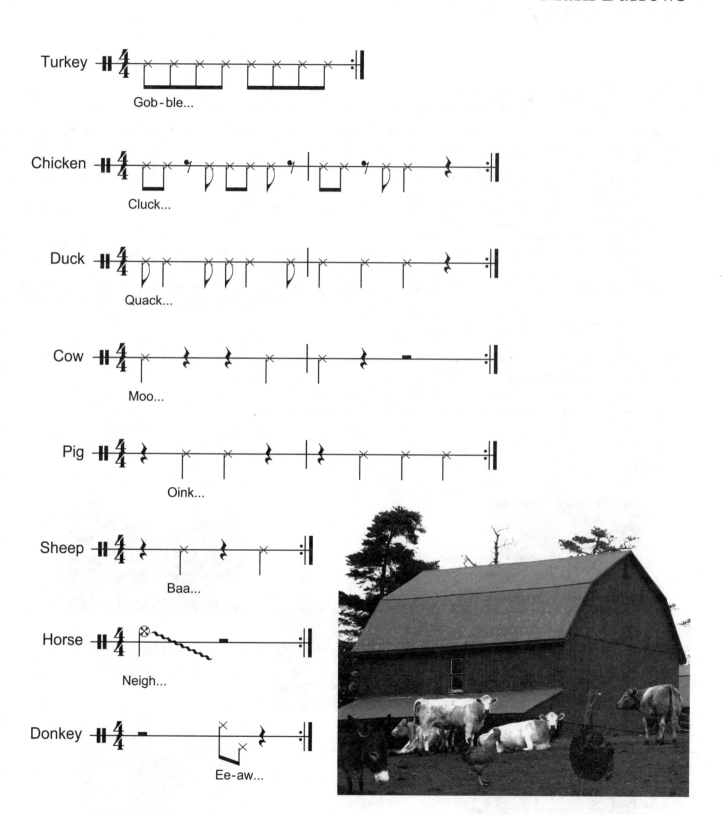

Click, Clap, Say, Stomp, Pop, and Pat:
The Whole Body Electric

Salutation Samba

Salutation Samba is based on the greetings of several languages. It may be performed as a speech percussion piece, or the rhythms may be performed with the suggested body percussion.

Swahili	*Jambo*	JAHM-bow
Hawaiian	*Aloha*	ah-LOW-ha
Spanish	*Hola*	O-lah
French	*Bonjour*	bawn-zure
Japanese	*Konichiwa*	koh-NEE-chee-wah

More salutations in different languages may be added to give the piece more texture. Other performance options include using the speech and body percussion simultaneously or alternating between speech and body percussion every four measures.

CD Information: The performance on the CD illustrates a way to combine speech and body percussion to create an extended performance piece. The form is:

A ⟶ Each spoken part is performed alone for 4 measures *(16 measures)*

B ⟶ All parts are spoken together, as written with repeat *(8 measures)*

C ⟶ Body percussion for all parts are performed together, as written with repeat *(8 measures)*

B ⟶ As before *(8 measures)*

Coda → All say "Hi" on final downbeat *(1 measure)*

Kenya

Spain

Hawaii

France

Japan

Salutation Samba

Mark Burrows

Planet Jam

Planet Jam is based on the names of the planets in our Solar System. This piece may be performed as speech percussion, using the names of the planets, or it may be performed using the suggested body percussion.

Process

1. Divide the students into groups and teach each group a different part.

2. Have one group start by chanting the "Mercury, Venus" part in rhythm.

3. Then add each of the other groups, moving from planets closest to the sun to those farthest away. (Ask your students which group should enter next according to this rule. If they don't know the order of the planets, teach a mnemonic device. One to try is: My Very Eager Mother Just Served Us Nine Pizzas.)

4. Once each part has entered, have them all chant together.

5. Next, cut each part off, starting with the "Mercury, Venus" part and moving farther away from the sun until the only part left is Pluto.

6. Rather than cut off the Pluto part, have it get softer and softer until all is silent.

Extension

Another performance option could be for the group chanting "Pluto" to use the Alternate Pluto part, shown below. You may remember from science class that Pluto's orbit is different from all the other planets'. The Alternate Pluto part reflects that eccentricity. While still written in $\frac{4}{4}$ time, "Pluto" is actually chanted every three beats.

This activity offers several cross-curricular extensions, including an exploration of Pluto's reclassification as a dwarf planet, as well as the discovery of other objects that are near Pluto. As scientists continue to study these icy objects, including one body called 2003 UB313, we may find ourselves living in a solar system that includes even more dwarf planets.

Planet Jam

Mark Burrows

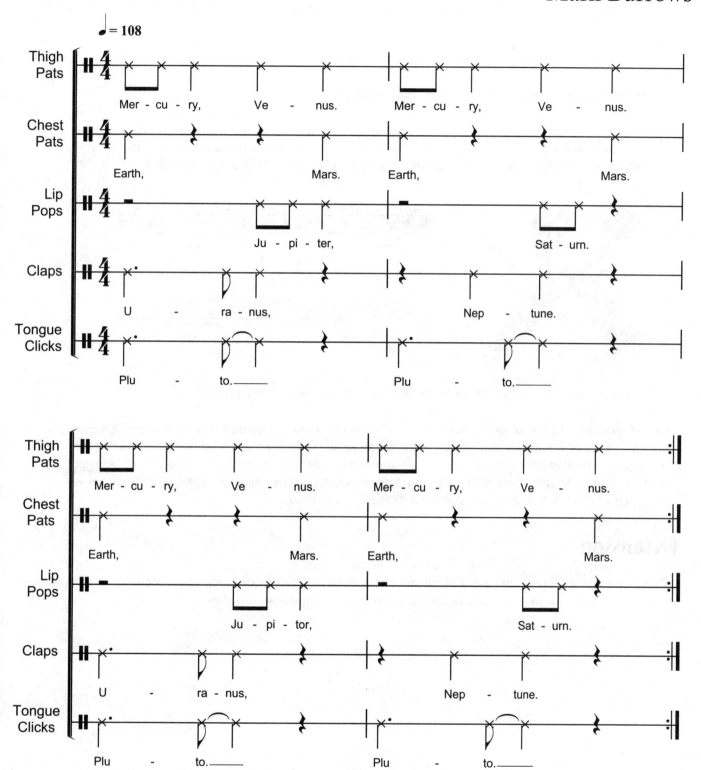

Body Percussion—Cuban

Body Percussion—Cuban uses a combination of body and mouth percussion. Each part is based on a traditional Cuban rhythm.

- The tongue clicks play the beat and represent the cowbell.

- The spoken "Tsh chk chk" represents the raspy guiro part.

- The claps represent the claves. Actually, the word clave has more than one meaning. Claves are two short, thick wooden sticks beat together in Latin American music. A clave is also a rhythmic pattern found in a lot of Latin American music. The two main claves, (3+2) and (2+3), are shown below.

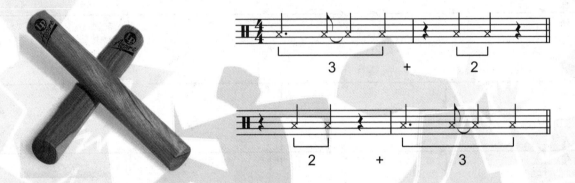

- The tummy and chest pats represent the congas, present in so much Cuban music.

CD Information: The recording of *Body Percussion—Cuban* provides a contrast to the layering performance option. Instead of varying texture, interest is created by dynamic change. After a one-measure introduction of tongue clicks, all parts enter together and perform the four-bar rhythm pattern four times. The dynamic then drops to *piano* and stays soft for one time through. Repeat and *crescendo* through all four measures to *forte*. Repeat two more times at *forte* and cue a strong final downbeat.

Extension

One performance option is to have the students play each of the parts while one student improvises a rhythm using claps with cupped hands. Give each student an opportunity to improvise a rhythm.

Body Percussion—Cuban

Mark Burrows

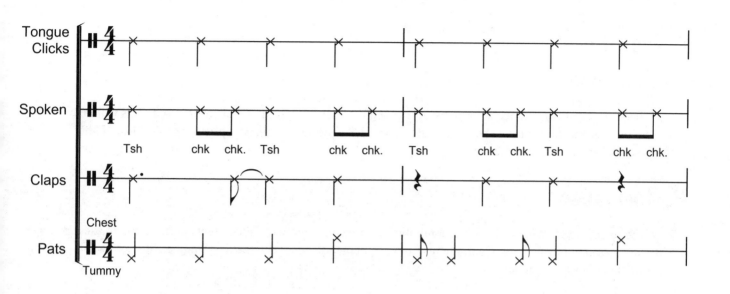

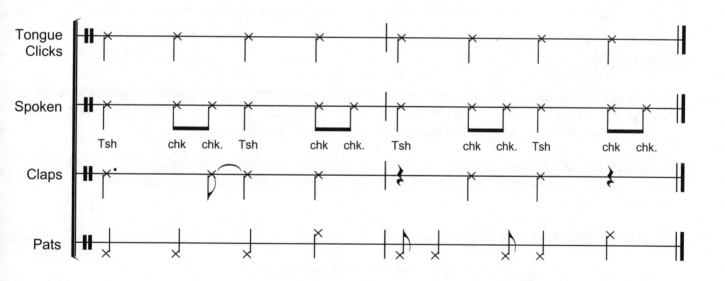

I Hear America Singing is a poem by the great American poet Walt Whitman (1819–1892). A tone poem is a musical depiction (usually orchestral) of a poem, story or other extra-musical idea. Let's put the two together.

Preparation

1. Teach each of the musical passages on page 38.

2. Divide the class into nine small groups. Assign eight of the groups a number from 1 to 8. This will be the passage each performs when you reach number 9. The remaining group will whistle "The Night Song" when you reach number 10.

Performance

Read the poem aloud. Wherever there is a number, stop reading and have all students perform the musical passage with the corresponding number. Continue reading the poem until you reach the next number. Students again perform that numbered musical example.

When you reach 9, you should continue reading the poem while students softly perform together their assigned passage. The goal is to create a blanket of sound with no underlying pulse. At number 10, you continue to read the poem, the students continue in their small groups, and group 10 is added to the mix.

Once the spoken poem is completed, have the students get louder until you give them a strong cutoff.

Extension

In order to make the full transition to tone poem (rather than a poem with accompaniment) the spoken word must be taken away, leaving only the musical depictions of the text. Divide the students into groups for each of the parts. Bring in and cutoff the various parts in the correct order to create a true tone poem.

In activities such as this, music and poetry form a symbiotic relationship. The words inspire our musical expression while the music helps us internalize the words of the poem. Here is a game that can further strengthen the bond between word and music.

- Have the students sit in a circle on the floor.

- Choose one student to stand and perform one of the musical passages.

- The others must guess the text portrayed by the musical passage.

- Give each student an opportunity to perform a musical passage.

I Hear America Singing

I hear America singing, the varied carols I hear, (1)

Those of mechanics, each one singing his as it
should be blithe and strong, (2)

The carpenter singing his as he measures his plank or beam, (3)

The mason singing his as he makes ready for work, or leaves off
work, (4)

The boatman singing what belongs to him in his boat, the deck-
hand singing on the steamboat deck; (5)

The shoemaker singing as he sits on his bench, the hatter singing as he stands; (6)

The wood-cutter's song, the ploughboy's on his way in the
morning, or at noon intermission or at sundown, (7)

The delicious singing of the mother, or of the young wife at
work, or of the girl sewing or washing, (8)

Each singing what belongs to him or her and to none else, (9)

The day what belongs to the day—at night, the party of young
fellows, robust, friendly, (10)

Singing, with open mouths, their strong melodious songs.

—Walt Whitman (1819-1892)

I Hear America Singing

Mark Burrows
Poem by Walt Whitman (1819-1892)

1. America the Beautiful

Vocalize on "Ah"

2. The Mechanic's Wrench

Krrrr - ik chk chk chk. Krrrr - ik chk chk. Krrrr -

3. The Carpenter's Saw

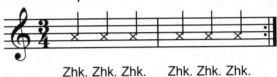

Zhk. Zhk. Zhk.   Zhk. Zhk. Zhk.

4. The Mason's Chisel

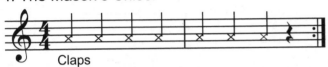

Claps

5. Steamboat Horn

Wah⎯⎯   Wah⎯⎯

6. The Shoemaker's Hammer

Light Tongue Clicks

7. The Woodcutter's Axe

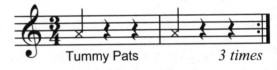

Tummy Pats   *3 times*

8. The Lullaby (*All the Pretty Little Horses*)

Hum

9. Perform all eight patterns together.

10. The Night Song (*Oh, Susanna*)

Whistle

The Body Electric

The Body Electric is an extended percussion piece utilizing many different sounds. There are three main sections:

- Section A, which incorporates the "Big Four" (stomps, pats, claps, and snaps).

- Section B, which highlights mouth percussion in the form of pops and clicks. (See "The Human Voice" on pages 16–17 for information on making these sounds.)

- Section C, which uses some of the softer sounds to give a change of pace.

The piece also includes an 8-bar coda that is the return of the A section. You may teach each of the parts/sections by rote, or reproduce the rhythms for each part (found on pages 43–44). You'll need to cue each section, and in some cases, each part within the section.

The sound suggestions for *The Body Electric* are just that—suggestions. Feel free to make whatever substitutions you like. Furthermore, feel free to make the piece longer, shorter, or even add more sounds or sections. (The performance on the CD is as written.)

This piece was written so that no more than four groups are needed (one group on each part). You may, however, decide to divide the students into smaller groups, with group changes coming at each new section.

The Body Electric

Mark Burrows

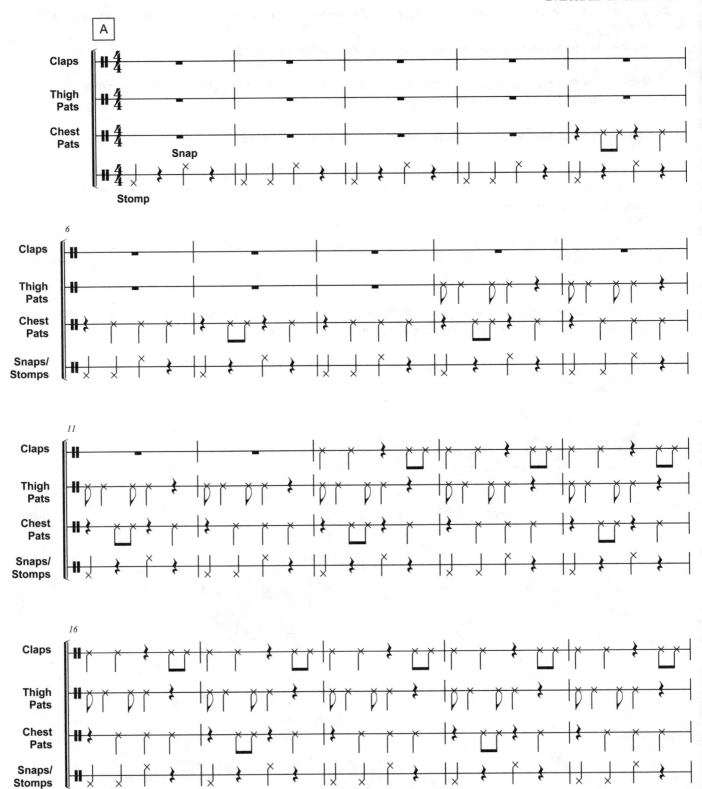

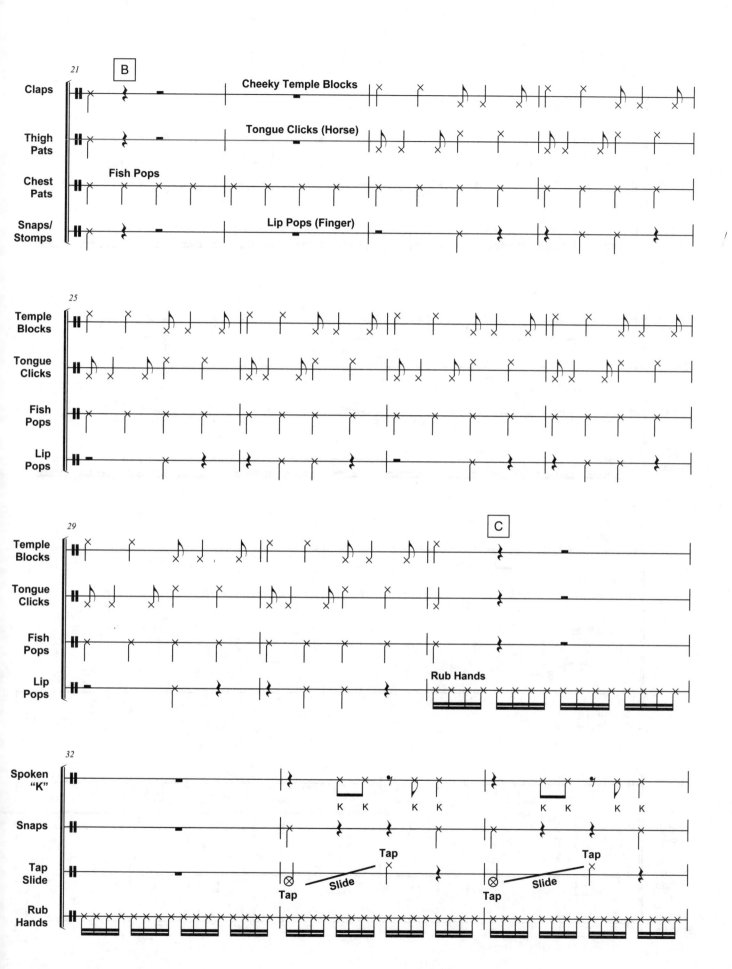

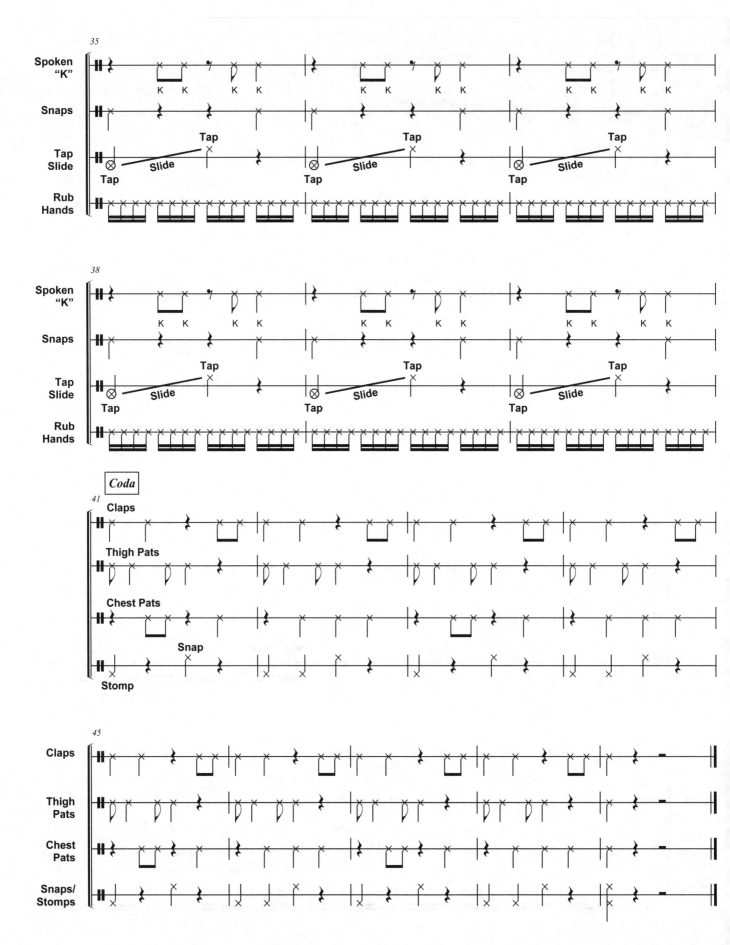

The Body Electric

Mark Burrows

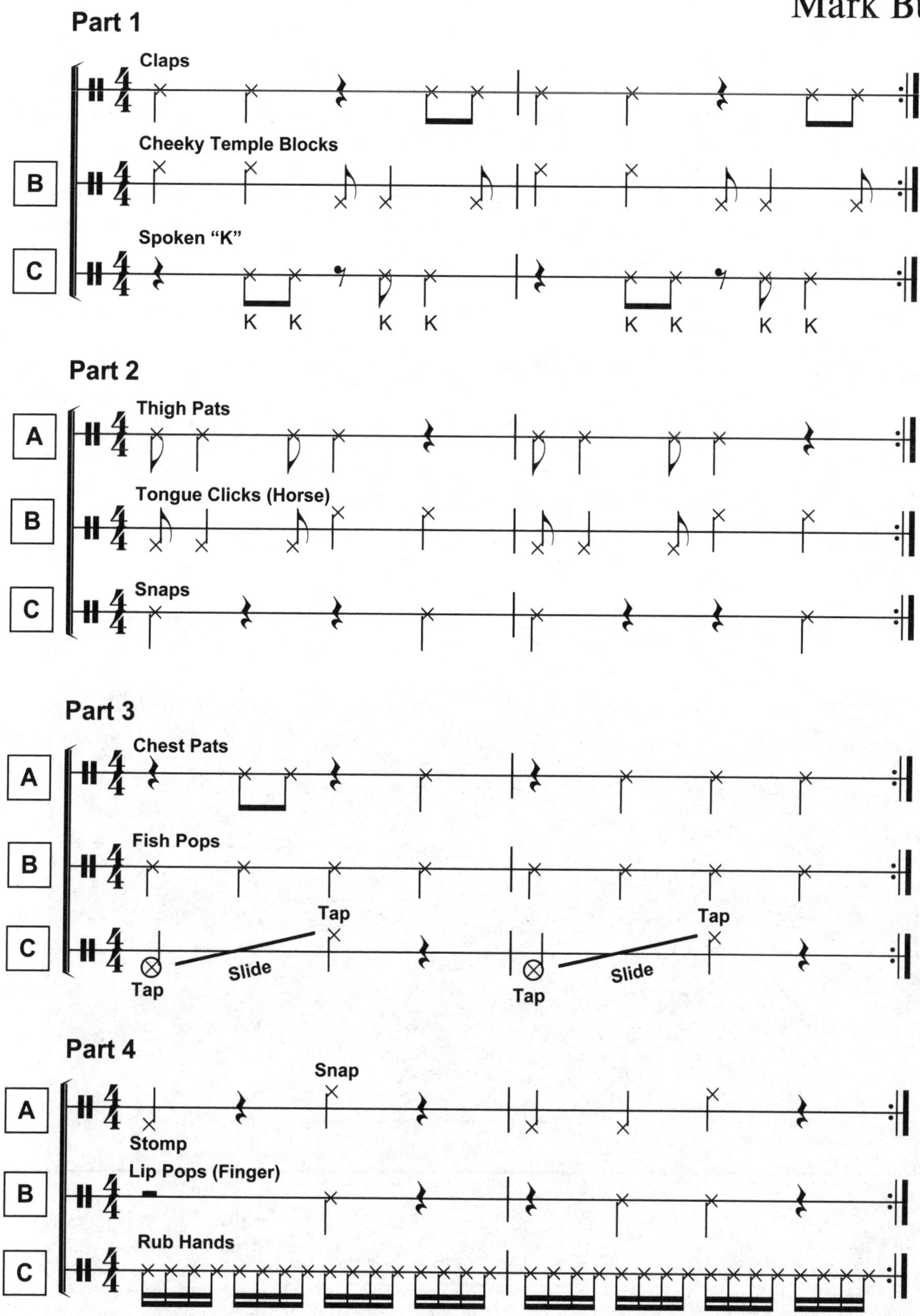

Part 1

Claps

B — Cheeky Temple Blocks

C — Spoken "K"

Part 2

A — Thigh Pats

B — Tongue Clicks (Horse)

C — Snaps

Part 3

A — Chest Pats

B — Fish Pops

C — Tap / Slide / Tap

Part 4

A — Snap

B — Stomp / Lip Pops (Finger)

C — Rub Hands

A Picture Is Worth a Thousand Sounds

Have you ever looked at a famous painting and wondered what the painting sounded like? Imagine standing on the Japanese footbridge in Monet's garden. What garden sounds could you hear? Could you hear the water rippling underneath the bridge? Could you hear a gentle breeze rustling the leaves of a nearby tree? Could you hear birds chirping in that same tree? Maybe even the painter himself could say something. (In Monet's case, it would most likely be in French.)

Find a famous painting (nature pictures and landscapes will work particularly well) and show it to the students. Have the students suggest body percussion and vocal/mouth sounds that could depict or accompany the visual images. In other words, have the students create a soundtrack for the painting.

Conduct a performance of this soundtrack. Make sure all the students are seated so they can see the picture.

- Start by assigning students to the different sounds and corresponding visual images.

- As you point to an image in the painting, have the students assigned to that image make the corresponding sound.

- The soundtrack could be created using the additive process—start with one part and continue to add parts, creating a rich texture of sounds. For more clarity, the soundtrack may be performed by having a part stop when a new one is brought in.

- Each part may have a specific rhythmic pattern, or it may be performed in free rhythmic style.

Classic Poems

For Younger Children

Twinkle, Twinkle

Twinkle, twinkle little star.
How I wonder what you are,
Up above the world so high,
Like a diamond in the sky.

—Traditional nursery rhyme

Pease Porridge

Pease porridge hot,
Pease porridge cold,
Pease porridge in the pot,
Nine days old.

Some like it hot.
Some like it cold.
Some like it in the pot,
Nine days old.

—Traditional nursery rhyme

Rub-a-dub Dub

Rub-a-dub dub,
Three men in a tub,
And who do you think they be?
The butcher, the baker,
The candlestick maker —
Roll them out, knaves all three.

—Traditional nursery rhyme

Five Little Monkeys

Five little monkeys jumping on the bed,
One fell off and bumped his head.
Mama called the doctor and the doctor said,
"No more monkeys jumping on the bed."

Four little monkeys...etc.

—Traditional fingerplay

Where Go the Boats?

Dark brown is the river,
  Golden is the sand.
It flows along for ever,
  With trees on either hand.

Green leaves a-floating,
  Castles of the foam,
Boats of mine a-boating—
  Where will all come home?

On goes the river
  And out past the mill,
Away down the valley,
  Away down the hill.

Away down the river,
  A hundred miles or more,
Other little children
  Shall bring my boats ashore.
      —*Robert Louis Stevenson (1850–1894)*

Los Pollitos

Los pollitos dicen, (lohs poh-YEE-tohs DEE-sehn)
"Pio, pio, pio," (PEE-oh, PEE-oh, PEE-oh)
Cuando tienen hambre, (KWAN-doh TYEHN-ehn AHM-breh)
Cuando tienen frio. (KWAN-doh TYEHN-ehn FREE-oh)

The little chicks say,
"Peep, peep, peep,"
When they are hungry,
When they are cold.
      —*Traditional Latin American*

For Older Children

Twinkle, Twinkle Little Bat

Twinkle, twinkle little bat!
How I wonder what you're at!
Up above the world you fly,
Like a tea-tray in the sky.
      —*From* Alice's Adventures in Wonderland, *by Lewis Carroll (1832–1898)*

Jabberwocky

'Twas brillig, and the slithy toves
Did gyre and gimble in the wabe;
All mimsy were the borogoves,
And the mome raths outgrabe.

'Beware the Jabberwock, my son!
The jaws that bite, the claws that catch!
Beware the Jubjub bird, and shun
The frumious Bandersnatch!'

He took his vorpal sword in hand:
Long time the manxome foe he sought—
So rested he by the Tumtum tree,
And stood awhile in thought.

And as in uffish thought he stood,
The Jabberwock, with eyes of flame,
Came whiffling through the tulgey wood,
And burbled as it came!

One, two! One, two! And through and through
The vorpal blade went snicker-snack!
He left it dead, and with its head
He went galumphing back.

'And hast thou slain the Jabberwock?
Come to my arms, my beamish boy!
O frabjous day! Callooh! Callay!'
He chortled in his joy.

'Twas brillig, and the slithy toves
Did gyre and gimble in the wabe;
All mimsy were the borogoves,
And the mome raths outgrabe.

—From Through the Looking-Glass and What Alice Found There, *by Lewis Carroll (1832-1898)*

Hope

"Hope" is the thing with feathers -
That perches in the soul -
And sings the tune without the words -
And never stops - at all -

And sweetest - in the Gale - is heard -
And sore must be the storm -
That could abash the little Bird
That kept so many warm -

I've heard it in the chillest land -
And on the strangest sea -
Yet, never, in Extremity,
It asked a crumb - of Me.

—Emily Dickinson (1830-1886)

The Eagle

He clasps the crag with crooked hands;
Close to the sun in lonely lands,
Ringed with the azure world, he stands.

The wrinkled sea beneath him crawls;
He watches from his mountain walls,
And like a thunderbolt he falls.

—Alfred, Lord Tennyson (1809-1892)

There Was a Young Lady Whose Nose

There was a young lady whose Nose
Continually prospers and grows;
When it grew out of sight,
She exclaimed in a fright,
"Oh! Farewell to the end of my Nose!"

—Edward Lear (1812-1888)

Hurt No Living Thing

Hurt no living thing:
Ladybird, no butterfly,
Nor moth with dusty wing,
No cricket chirping cheerily,

Nor grasshopper so light of leap,
Nor dancing gnat, no beetle fat,
Nor harmless worms that creep.

—Christina Rossetti (1830-1894)